Kids love reading
Choose Your Own Adventure®!

"It was cool how you got to make your own choices. Reading *Choose Your Own Adventure* helped me picture the stories and made reading them a lot more exciting."
Gregg Skowronski, age 10

"I love *Choose Your Own Adventure*, it's like 40 books in one!"
Hannah Marion, age 13

"You don't have to worry about the characters making bad decisions. The author doesn't choose the ending, you do."
Patrick Meany, age 11

"The author made me feel like I was in the character's shoes. I loved being able to choose how the book ends!"
Addy Dettor, age 12

Watch for these titles coming up in the
Choose Your Own Adventure® series.

Ask your bookseller for books you have missed
or visit us at cyoa.com to learn more.

THE LOST JEWELS
OF NABOOTI

BY R. A. MONTGOMERY

ILLUSTRATED BY
T. KORNMANEEROJ, K. CHANCHAREON,
S. BUTSINGKHON, AND A. UTAHIGARN

CHOOSE YOUR OWN ADVENTURE® CLASSICS
A DIVISION OF

CHOOSECO
WAITSFIELD, VERMONT

Lost Jewels of Nabooti ©1982 R. A. Montgomery,
Warren, Vermont. All Rights Reserved.

Artwork, design, and revised text ©2005 Chooseco LLC,
Waitsfield, Vermont. All Rights Reserved.

Concurrently published by Sundance Publishing,
Northborough, MA as *Lost Jewels of Nafouti*

Illustrated by: V. Pornkerd, S. Yaweera, & J. Donploypetch
Book design: Stacey Hood, Big Eyedea Visual Design
Chooseco dragon logos designed by: Suzanne Nugent

For information regarding permission, write to:

CHOOSECO

P.O. Box 46
Waitsfield, Vermont 05673
www.cyoa.com

ISBN 10 1-933390-44-1
ISBN 13 978-1-933390-44-4

Published simultaneously in the United States and Canada

Printed in the United States

0 9 8 7 6 5 4

This book is dedicated to Ramsey and Anson

And to Shannon

BEWARE and WARNING!

This book is different from other books.

You and YOU ALONE are in charge of what happens in this story.

There are dangers, choices, adventures and consequences. YOU must use all your numerous talents and much of your enormous intelligence. The wrong decision could end in disaster—even death. But, don't despair. At anytime, YOU can go back and make another choice, alter the path of your story, and change its result.

You are about to embark on a search with your cousins Peter and Lucy. Jewels with powers almost beyond human imagining have disappeared from a museum show in Paris. Or did the jewels ever even make it out of Africa? And what does your Uncle have to do with it? It's time to buckle down to some good old-fashioned detective work.

But watch your back!

Halfway through your summer vacation you get an urgent telegram from your cousins Peter and Lucy:

NEED YOUR HELP FINDING THE JEWELS OF NABOOTI. FLY TO BOSTON AT ONCE. BRING PASSPORT. DANGER, BE CAREFUL.
PETER AND LUCY

After reading the telegram several times, you are still puzzled. You remember the jewels; who could forget them? The two diamonds shone like the sun's reflection off a glacier, and the two rubies were like the eyes of a jungle creature at night. Peter's father had bought them from a trader in Morocco many years ago.

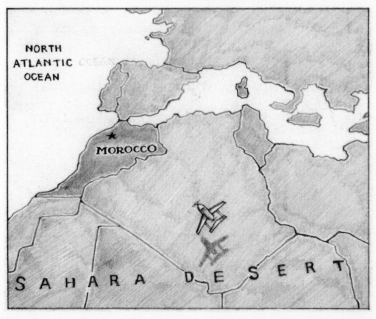

Turn to the next page.

2

The trader had been nervous about the sale but also anxious to get rid of the jewels. Two days later, Peter's father had returned to the Casbah to ask more about the jewels only to find the stall closed. A small sign announced the sad and unfortunate death of the stall owner, a Mr. Abdul Said. That same day, he received a letter at his hotel demanding the return of the jewels. The letter warned him that his life was in danger if he did not return them. He ignored the letter, but he always hinted about the strange and mysterious powers the stones held.

Peter and Lucy tell you the jewels have been stolen from a museum show in Paris. What can you do to help your cousins find them? You pack your bags and leave your house in New Orleans and fly to Boston. You glance over your shoulder, nervously searching for followers.

Peter and Lucy meet you at the airport.

"We don't have much time," Peter announces. "If you agree to help, take the plane to Paris tomorrow afternoon. From Paris you'll fly to Morocco. You'll have to hurry."

Turn to page 4.

4

"But, Peter," you complain, "I don't understand what this is all about."

"You will when you read this letter. Here."

It reads:

The Jewels of Nabooti are four keys to the hidden wisdom and wealth of a secret African tribe. Those who have the jewels either enjoy health and fame or they suffer agony beyond belief. The current owners of the jewels must guard against their being lost or stolen. They must wait to hand them over to the appointed messengers of Nabooti. Loss of the jewels could mean DEATH.

You are puzzled by the letter. Peter and Lucy try to reassure you. But the truth is that their lives have been threatened if they continue to search for the jewels. They have asked you to search for the jewels because you are unknown to the thieves. You will be relatively safe, as safe as anyone can be on the trail of the Jewels of Nabooti.

If you agree to go on tomorrow's plane for Paris, go on to the next page.

If you demand more time, information, and extra help, turn to page 9.

"Fasten your seat belts, put your seatbacks in an upright position, turn off all electronic devices. Flight 231 for Paris is now ready for takeoff." The flight attendant explains about emergency procedures, but you listen with only half an ear. Then there is the roar of the jet engines as the plane rushes down the runway and leaps into the air.

Turning away from the small plane window, you notice that the person sitting next to you is doodling on a pad. Long, narrow fingers grasp the gold pen tightly. They are a bloodless white. What is creepier still is that they have no nails! You sneak a closer look at his face and see eyes that reflect no light, a thin mouth showing no lines at the corners, and a closely shaven jaw. A mustache hides a scar that runs from the nostril to the corner of the mouth. You look down and see that the scribbles on the pad are diamond-shaped. They seem to spell out the word "NABOOTI." A shiver of fear races through you. This cannot be a coincidence! The person next to you certainly knows who you are. He, too, must be looking for the missing jewels.

Go on to page 7.

Fatigue overcomes your fear, and you fall into a troubled sleep. When you waken, you are over the English Channel descending toward Paris.

"Would you care to share a taxi into Paris, my friend?" It is the man next to you. You start at his words as though a knife were tickling the back of your neck.

"Why, I, I . . . don't know. Where are you going?" It is a pretty lame way to delay your answer, but you need to do some fast thinking.

The stranger fixes you with an eerie stare and says, "We are searching for the same thing. I need your help and you need mine."

You have a sudden vision of a strange man beckoning you into his taxi.

If you accept his offer for the cab ride,
turn to page 8.

If you make excuses and refuse his help,
turn to page 12.

A row of taxis meets you at the entrance to the airport. You and your strange companion jump in one and roar off to the center of Paris.

The ride is fast and dangerous. Your driver doesn't seem to think that there are any rules to the road.

Then you are standing on the sidewalk in front of a small cafe. Your companion motions to a waiter inside and tells you, "One moment, all is ready."

The waiter scurries away only to return a minute later with two glasses and a note asking you to meet a man named Molotawa at the table in the back of the restaurant.

"He is our contact here in Paris. Listen to what he says. But be careful. Watch the doors and windows. Our enemies are about."

If you take a seat on the left near the door, turn to page 16.

If you sit with your back to the wall, turn to page 18.

"Hey, I can't just hop on another plane. I just don't know enough about what is happening."

Peter looks at you and shrugs his shoulders.

"I don't blame you. Let's go back to my house."

You take a long, roundabout route to his house to shake off followers.

That night over dinner the story of the jewels comes out. Peter says, "Three times in recent years messages have come demanding their return to the Nabooti tribe. Our father refused to be frightened into returning the jewels."

Lucy quickly adds, "It wasn't just that they were worth a small fortune. Dad believed in the legends about the jewels. He knew the jewels had strange and magical powers."

"And of course then he was killed in that tragic accident," Peter reminds you.

You remember the details of that awful event. Your uncle was stepping onto a sailboat from a dock on a perfectly calm day, when the boat suddenly moved. Your uncle slipped between the boat and the dock and was crushed. And his last words to Peter and Lucy were "Protect the jewels at all costs."

Go on to page 10.

10

Peter was spooked by his father's words. A short time after, he received a note directing him to deliver the jewels to a rug merchant in Tangiers, a Moroccan city.

"Before I had a chance, three men broke into the house, bound me hand and foot, and stole the jewels," he finishes.

CRASH! As you and your cousins talk, the window is shattered by a shotgun blast. No one is hurt, but you are all terrified.

A musical chime plays, and Peter, shaking, scrambles for the phone. "That's strange, no one but my family knows this number."

When he picks it up a deep voice says, "Give up now or else. This is just a warning." Click. The phone goes dead.

A wind blows in the trees outside the broken window. The three of you stare at each other.

If you want to give up now, turn to page 15.

If you decide to go in search of the Jewels of Nabooti, turn to page 14.

12

A large crowd gives you the perfect opportunity to escape. Deciding to avoid your companion, you duck into a phone booth. The crowd swirls around you, and he is gone. Slowly you open the door, look cautiously around, and step out onto the airport waiting room floor.

There is a tap on your shoulder.

You spin around. Standing there is a tall woman with intense eyes and a muscular midget in a tracksuit. He has a small laptop with him.

"Come with us. We are going to help you with the Jewels of Nabooti," the woman announces.

Too much! No matter where you go, they are after you. Is there no escape?

"OK, OK, what is it? What do you know?"

She looks at you and then says, "There is a jet waiting over in the private air terminal. It will take you to Morocco. Here is your identification." She hands you a small sliver of ivory with a design on it. "Whoever sees it will give you help. Good luck."

The midget grins in an evil way. He opens up the laptop so you can look inside. It's not a laptop at all. It contains a dagger with a sharp point. The dagger sends you a different kind of message than the kind you get over the Internet.

A very different message.

If you go to the jet, turn to page 19.

If you tell them that there must be some mistake and drift off into the crowd, turn to page 20.

14

You look at Peter and Lucy for a long time. Then as if someone else were speaking for you, you tell them, "I can't do it. We'll all get killed. Give up. Get the police. Let them handle it."

Silence. Peter and Lucy both look away. Finally, Peter speaks, "But you've got to help us. You're our only hope."

"OK! But it's too big for us." You hesitate to turn down your cousins who sound desperate. "Wait a minute. Maybe I can get Beech Muzzwell to help. Beech is an adventurer, a private detective, and a good person to have around in an emergency."

If you get in touch with Muzzwell and he agrees to go, turn to page 24.

If Muzzwell is nowhere to be found, turn to page 28.

Rising from your safe position on the floor, you head for the front door, slipping on the shotgun pellets on the smooth floor. You make it to the door, but whoever was out there is gone. You are silhouetted in the doorway—definitely a bad place to be—but nothing happens.

"Peter, they are dead serious. If you don't get the jewels back, they will kill you and Lucy. I'll help. I'll leave for Paris tomorrow."

Peter and Lucy gather around you slapping you on the back and shaking your hand. You seem to have forgotten the shotgun blast and the telephone call—but then the merriment is broken by the ring of the phone.

When you pick it up, you hear a voice say, "We weren't kidding. Next time you won't be so lucky." Click! The connection is broken again.

If you decide to leave without getting the aid of the police, turn to page 22.

If you get in touch with the police, turn to page 21.

A tall, black man wearing a red, green, and black African shirt enters the room. He looks like an athlete, and he quickly takes a seat at a round table. It is Molotawa. He begins to clean his fingernails with a sharp, long-bladed knife, and he does not even look up when you slip into the seat next to him.

You survey the room. Any one of the customers could mean trouble for you. You must be prepared to make a quick escape. Your friend from the airplane has disappeared. Where did he go?

Molotawa speaks, "I am from the Nabooti group. We believe in world peace, knowledge and wisdom, and the end to all wars. We are an ancient group, and we have fought long and hard for our goal of peace. The jewels when in place give us a special power to stop people who oppose peace. Do you understand?"

You puzzle over what he says. But just when you are about to speak, someone at a nearby table jumps to his feet and lunges forward. There is a knife in his hand.

If you race for the nearest exit, turn to page 27.

If you grab a chair to defend yourself, turn to page 29.

You remember reading somewhere that it is safest if you sit with your back to the wall. That way no one can sneak up on you from behind.

The waiter hovers over your table for a minute taking your order. Then Molotawa appears—at least you assume that it is Molotawa—and takes a seat next to you. He is a handsome man of about twenty-five years of age. There are tribal scars on his cheeks, two rows of three lines each. The multicolored African shirt fits loosely over his frame.

"Thank you for agreeing to meet with me. It's good that you came. Perhaps we can recover the lost jewels with each other's help."

You nod in general agreement. "But who are you?"

Molotawa looks at you for a moment, and then says, "I am a prince of the ancient Nabooti tribe. We ruled a large region of Africa for many, many years before Africa was taken by European countries. We were fair and just. The jewels are a powerful symbol of our leadership. They have magic powers. They can confuse the evildoers and stop the bad. We must have them back to continue our work."

You are impressed with his words and his princely bearing.

"If you wish, you can meet my father, the king, here in Paris, or you can go now to Senegal where my people are."

If you want to meet Molotawa's father, turn to page 34.

If you decide to go to Senegal, turn to page 30.

A beautiful and unusual jet plane sits in readiness at the private air terminal. It has silver and yellow wings and a bright red body. You are met by two large men in business suits. "Follow us. Be quiet."

There is no opportunity for hesitation or argument. They hustle you into the aircraft.

The passenger area is small and crowded. The two men sit next to each other and face you.

"Alpha Omega, 234, cleared for takeoff." It is the control tower speaking. Then you are up and away. Paris below looks like a small town or even a play city in a sandbox.

Soon you are at cruising altitude flying over the Pyrenees, across Spain, then the coast of Africa looms under you.

Puffs of smoke from the wheels hitting the runway at almost 250 kph announce your arrival in Morocco. No one has said a word. You know no more than when you left Boston, except that quite a few people are on your trail.

There are no friendly faces. There is no escape.

Turn to page 32.

20

"I'm sorry, this must be a mistake. You have the wrong person. I don't know anything about Jewels of . . . . What did you say the name was . . . Jewels of Natusi or Magoosy?"

The woman looks at you with a puzzled expression. She pulls out a small whistle and blows it. It is a silent whistle, designed for dogs. Within seconds, you are surrounded by French police and hustled off to a small room where you are questioned for two hours. They accuse you of being a smuggler.

"But, I've never smuggled anything in my life. Search me."

The two police officers on either side of you do a quick but complete search. Amazing—in a jacket pocket they discover a small packet. When it is opened you are shocked to see a very large uncut diamond!

"So, you are not a smuggler. Well, well, what do we have here? This is a mere nothing, eh? You know smuggling such diamonds from countries in Africa is an international crime. What do you have to say for yourself now?"

If you tell them about the Jewels of Nabooti, turn to page 37.

If you ask to call the American embassy for legal help, turn to page 40.

At the police station you find a sergeant behind the desk. He looks up and says, "OK, whaddaya want?"

It does not inspire confidence in you. You hastily explain the circumstances. The bored voice says, "What are you, some kind of a kook? You putting me on about jewels and Africa and all that bunk?"

You groan. Oh well, you might as well go it on your own. But, maybe you should get someone to help you. Maybe Anson and Ramsey who have helped you before can help you again. You need good friends at a time like this, people you can trust.

Give them a call by turning to page 42.

"I don't think we need the police in this matter. They could just cause us more trouble. Let's go it alone," says Lucy.

You agree. For the rest of the evening and into early morning the three of you huddle together in talk. You glance nervously toward doors and windows. You are afraid of another attack.

"Time to go now. Hurry. We will get you to the airport and meet you later when you want us."

Driving in early morning traffic, it is hard to tell whether or not you are being followed. You think you see a light-colored compact car darting in and out of the traffic flow in an attempt to follow you, but you can't be sure.

When you get to the check-in counter for the international flight to Paris, three squarely built men with crew cuts stand by the counter watching the door. You slip by them and go to another airline.

What do you do now?

Go on to the next page.

If you continue on the flight to Paris, turn to page 39.

If you escape these three people by booking a flight to Spain instead of France, turn to page 41.

Peter and Lucy are not happy with the delay involved in getting Beech Muzzwell to Boston. Yet, you are convinced that Muzzwell is essential to your success.

Over a lunch of tacos and refried beans, the three of you discuss the problems of the global search for the lost jewels. The telephone's ring interrupts the calm of the moment.

"Hello, this is the FBI calling. We are sorry to report that a Mr. Beech Muzzwell has been kidnapped from the East Side Air Terminal in New York by a gang of jewel thieves. A note was left with one of the bus drivers saying that he will be killed if you continue your search for the Jewels of Nabooti. I think we had better get together for a talk. I'll send a car out for you right away."

"That's it. It is too much for us. Let's quit while we're still alive."

Peter and Lucy look at you and nod in agreement.

The End

Just as you reach the exit someone shouts, "Stop that man! He's a thief!" Hands reach out to grab you; one of the waiters stands right in your way. You dodge around him successfully and make it to the street.

Which way do you go? Before you have a chance to decide, your question is answered for you. The man from the plane beckons to you from an open car door.

"Get in, we don't have much time."

People are coming out of the restaurant shouting for the police. But, what is really going on? Maybe you would be better off on your own.

If you get into the car, turn to page 44.

If you run on by, ignoring the man in the car, turn to page 64.

Beech Muzzwell is reportedly climbing in the Hindu Kush mountains with an international team of alpinists.

There is no way to reach him. Time is running out. You had better be on your way to Paris. Peter and Lucy rush you to the airport.

Go back to page 5.

The man falls on his face choking on a piece of meat. The knife in his hand rattles harmlessly on the floor. He struggles for air, his face getting redder by the moment. Two waiters rush up. One grabs him around the middle of the chest with both arms, gives a violent squeeze, and his windpipe is cleared of the steak. The man begins to breathe. The excitement is over—for the moment. You are safe for now. But you're embarrassed standing there holding the chair like a lion tamer. Fortunately no one is looking at you.

You sit down again, and to your surprise a stranger is sitting next to Molotawa. He is about to speak to you.

Turn to page 126.

30

Senegal, a beautiful country on Africa's Atlantic coast, was a French colony until its independence almost fifty years ago. It has been relatively peaceful with a healthy economy.

You soon find yourself in Dakar, the busy and colorful capital of this West African country.

"Come with me, my friend. Here in Dakar you will be safe. All the people know of the Jewels of Nabooti. We will be helped whenever we ask for it."

Just as you enter the Grand Hotel, a siren shrieks, and both of you spin about to see a car scream around the corner. It's headed right for the hotel. Only there is a problem. There is no one in it. It smashes into the hotel lobby and barely misses you and Molotawa.

Was this an accident? If you think it was, turn to page 50.

If you think it was not an accident, turn to page 48.

32

A black Mercedes limousine pulls up to the jet. A powerfully built man in dark clothes stands by the car holding the door open. You are moved along with little or no choice to escape or even to ask what is going on.

How strange it is that no one talks to you. Maybe this is their plan to make you nervous. If it is, they are succeeding brilliantly. It is like waiting in a dentist's office to be called in for your appointment. The minutes seem to be unreal and painfully long. When you open your mouth to speak, you find that no words come out.

Tires screech around corners. The car speeds toward town, past rolling hills filled with brilliant yellow, blue, and red flowers. You catch a glimpse of the turquoise sea from one hilltop. Soon you are in the middle of Tangiers. Alongside modern cars, buildings, and people in western clothes are donkeys, hand-drawn carts, and people wearing the ancient robes and colorful costumes of North Africa.

When will someone talk to you? This is maddening. The limousine threads its way through narrow streets. It then stops in the shadow of the wall of the Medina—the great walled inner city of Tangiers with its winding streets, dark tunnel-like paths, and exotic sounds and smells. The two of you start off on foot.

Go on to page 35.

Unfortunately, you never meet with Molotawa's father. While waiting for the Metro (subway) to take you across Paris to the king, two men posing as street musicians push you off the platform. You fall onto the third rail. Electrocuted. It's all over for you. Too bad!

The End

The driver points to a small opening in the Medina wall. A blind woman sits by the opening, begging. When you walk by her, she spits at your feet. You jump back in disgust, but the driver just keeps pushing you on.

In your pocket is the small ivory identification piece given to you in Paris as a sign that can be used to get help. You stop and pretend to tie your shoe. You look at the blind woman, and you're sure she winked at you. Was that just a tic, or maybe she's not blind and trying to signal you?

Turn to page 36.

The ivory piece will bring you help. How badly do you need help now? Should you give the token to the blind woman, or should you save it until later?

If you give the ivory piece to the blind woman,
turn to page 49.

If you decide to keep it for now and use it later,
turn to page 52.

"Captain, let me explain. Give me a chance. This is all a dreadful mistake. I need your help."

The police captain looks at you, and a knowing smile crosses his face.

"We are always here to help. What help do you require?" You don't like the tone of his remark.

"It's about the Jewels of Nabooti."

The captain, who has been toying with a pen, drops it to the floor as though it were red-hot.

"The Jewels of Nabooti?" He looks across to the other officers in the room. "The Jewels of Nabooti! What a curse they are to all who are involved with them. What do you know about them?"

You're nervous, but you try to keep your cool. You tell the police that you suspect that the diamond was slipped into your pocket by someone who is trying to frame you.

Turn to the next page.

It's a far-fetched story, but the police captain seems to believe you. To make sure, he calls Interpol, the international police. He jabbers in French, nodding his head. You understand what he says but don't let on. Then he turns to you and says: "Interpol tells me that you are telling the truth. We would like to help you. The Jewels of Nabooti are powerful, and those who seek them can be dangerous. If you would like, we can provide you with a plainclothes detective. Or if you would prefer to go on to Morocco alone, we can give you a special phone number to call if danger threatens."

If you accept the offer of police protection, turn to page 53.

If you travel to Morocco alone, but accept the special phone number, turn to page 54.

Running the risk of going on the Paris flight doesn't work out. The three men surround you, and one of them jabs a needle with a knockout drug into your arm.

When you wake up, you are in a cabin deep in a forested area surrounded by low hills. Your hands and feet are securely bound. You are cold and stiff and hungry. A large poisonous snake creeps out of a pile of leaves and heads for you. There is nothing you can do. It's all over.

The End

40

The American embassy sends over a member of the legal staff. You tell her the long, complicated story. Her advice is to return to the United States as quickly as possible. She will do her best to get the French police to release you.

"The Jewels of Nabooti are too dangerous for you to retrieve alone. Let them be."

You feel depressed, but you are also convinced that there are too many people involved for you to handle. You follow her advice, give up the chase, and return to the United States.

The End

A loudspeaker blares out the message: "Air Iberia is in its final boarding phase. All passengers proceed to Gate 14."

You make up your mind to go. With the money Peter and Lucy gave you, you buy a ticket and proceed to Gate 14. Now and again you glance over your shoulder to watch the people at the Air France counter. Obviously they don't know you, or they would have followed you.

Off to Spain.

Once there, you can either fly up to Paris to begin the search or you can fly to Morocco and search for the rug merchant that Peter and Lucy told you about.

If you go up to Paris according to Peter and Lucy's plan, turn to page 57.

If you decide to skip Paris, and head directly for Morocco, turn to page 58.

"Hello, yes, this is Anson. No, Ramsey isn't here. Oh hi, I recognized your voice. I haven't heard from you all summer."

You quickly get over the talk about what you are doing and sketch in the details of the missing jewels and your search.

"Will you guys come with me? I really need your help."

Anson doesn't hesitate a moment. He agrees to meet you and join in the search. Ramsey is on a secret mission in the Himalayas and unable to come.

Anson wants to meet you in Morocco. You would prefer meeting him in Paris because you want to stick to Peter and Lucy's plan.

If you agree to meet him in Morocco, turn to page 55.

If you pressure him to meet you in Paris, turn to page 60.

The smallest of the three—a man with a scar running horizontally across his forehead, a heavy beard, squinty eyes, and nervous gestures—speaks.

"You have exactly thirty-six seconds by my digital watch to decide to come with us or not. If you don't, the price is high. We will extinguish you. If you do, who knows what will happen?"

The driver secretly slips you a pistol. Now you have a choice.

Go peacefully with them by turning to page 61.

Fight it out by turning to page 62.

44

Your hesitation is enough. The man in the car reaches out and grabs you by the arm; he holds a gun in his other hand. Before you know it, you are in the car threading your way through Paris traffic.

"Duck down so no one sees you. I'll put this blanket over your head." You don't really have a choice so you obey. The car accelerates, and you instinctively know that you must be on a super highway heading out of Paris—but where are you going?

After almost fifteen minutes, the man from the plane tells you that you may sit up. The danger has passed.

You were right; the car is speeding away from Paris in an easterly direction.

Then there is the sound of helicopter rotor blades beating down on you. You see a four-place Bell executive helicopter in the sky. Three people including the pilot peer out the Plexiglas windows surveying your car. The helicopter does a complete turnaround and ends up in front of your racing car.

You see the muzzle of a machine gun poke through the small window opening in the chopper's side. The roar of the machine gun is lost in the rotor noise. But the bullets are real enough. They rip through the thin metal of the car miraculously missing the driver, you, and the man from the airplane. The car is finished, however, and skids to a sloppy stop near the embankment on the left.

The helicopter lands and the three men jump out with guns drawn.

There is nothing you can do—for the moment.

Go back to page 43.

46

Playing it safe, aren't you? Double back, seek Raoul, but in the end, give up the chase for these fabled gems. You will never find them. TOO BAD.

The End

You leave the house and step out onto a narrow street. A man with long hair and a beard stops you.

"Need a guide? I know Morocco very well. Very cheap."

How lucky. He can help you find the rug merchant. You tell him the address of the rug merchant. You never wrote it down. Peter and Lucy had you memorize it.

The second you tell him the address, three men step out of a doorway. They are your captors. They've double-crossed you. They didn't fall for your bluff for a second. One of the men levels a gun at you and fires.

Zap! You lose.

The End

This was a phony accident if you ever saw one. Two policemen arrive and explain that it was a terrible mistake. The police driver stepped out of the car and forgot to put on the emergency brake, they say. They are embarrassed, and they apologize for the accident.

You are not satisfied with the quick explanation and apology. Something is wrong. You decide to examine the wrecked car.

Turn to page 50.

Instinct tells you to give the ivory piece to the beggar. You drop it into her outstretched hands.

The moment the ivory piece is in her hands, she yells, "AIEEE!" Two short, wiry men in hooded robes step out of a small door in the wall.

One of them shouts in English, "We are your friends, follow us." The other man wrestles with the huge man who drove the limousine.

For a moment you half decide to run away, and then you go with them through dark tunnels and streets deep into the Medina. You haven't the faintest idea where you are or what is going on. The ivory piece seems to have a strange and powerful effect on these people.

"In here." It is your new guide speaking.

Seated at a small table is an old man with white hair and beard. He is smoking from a water pipe. Rugs are everywhere—hanging on the walls, rolled up and stacked in piles. Could this be the rug merchant that Peter and Lucy talked about?

"Sit down, do not be frightened," says your new guide. You sit.

"We have followed your trip from Boston. We know who you are, and we want the jewels. Now give them to us."

"But, I don't have the jewels," you protest.

The old man rises and looks sharply at you. "Look in the pocket of your coat."

If you decide to obey him, turn to page 74.

If you decide to run for the door, turn to page 76.

You cross the lobby to the car and open the car door. Pinned to the steering wheel is a note with your name on it! It reads:

WE WON'T GIVE UP. GO BACK WHERE YOU BELONG.

There is a sign of two crosses at the bottom.

You are not sure just what it means, but you are sure that it spells nothing good for you. This was certainly no accident.

The moment you leave the hotel, you are surrounded by police officers who claim that this police car was stolen only minutes before. One of them says, "The

note is addressed to you. You must come with us to police headquarters. Stealing an official car is serious business."

You protest, but they refuse to listen to you. Off you go to see the commissioner of police. Should you tell them about the lost jewels or should you pretend that you know nothing? You decide to come clean and tell the whole story.

The chief of police listens politely to your story. He tells you that he, too, believes in the Jewels of Nabooti and that he will help you recover them. "Allow me to introduce you to my aide, Ouobessa Soul-One, a Senegalese from the North by the Senegal River."

You shake hands with Ouobessa. He presents you with three options in your quest.

You can consult a shaman on page 68;

or you can try to contact the Nabooti tribe direct by going to page 70;

or you can search in Dakar by going to page 72.

It's too late to do anything. The huge man rushes you along the twisting streets of the Medina. You enter a small square and come to a halt at an open stall selling olives and spices. There is a brief muffled conversation between your guide and the proprietor of the stall. Then you are pushed through a door in the back of the stall. The door leads to a tunnel that in turn leads to the yacht basin in the harbor.

"Don't move. We will take care of everything." The accent is French, and the voice is harsh.

A powerboat nestles against the dock. The rocking motion of the waves makes its sharp snout resemble a shark. You are hustled aboard. Two crewmen start the motor, the lines are cast off, and with a roar of the engines the boat nudges out into the harbor.

Throttles are pushed full forward. The boat leaps on top of the waves and speeds toward Cap Spartel and the Pillars of Hercules.

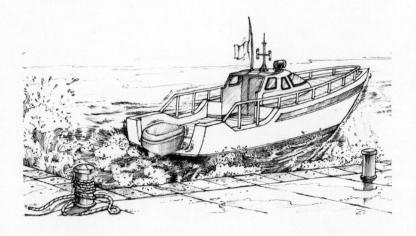

Turn to page 128.

A small, thin, nervous-looking person is called in. They introduce him as Raoul Thierry—special detective in the smuggling and international crime division of the French Sûreté. He works with Interpol, the worldwide police network cooperating with almost all countries in the pursuit of criminals.

Raoul says little, but you are glad to have him with you.

You sit alone with him working out a plan of action. He says, "This could be my most interesting and perhaps my most dangerous case. Would you like to carry a gun? Perhaps you will need it."

If you accept the offer of a weapon, turn to page 75.

If you refuse to be armed because you do not believe in guns or killing, turn to page 78.

What good are a bunch of telephone numbers if you are in real danger? But you want freedom of movement. You would rather rely on your friends Anson, Ramsey, or Beech Muzzwell to help you than the Moroccan police. Yet, it is comforting to know that there could be help at the end of the phone.

The trip from Paris to Morocco is uneventful. Now you walk about this half-European, half-North African city trying to decide on your next move. Of course you have the address of a contact in the marketplace. You decide you can't hesitate.

The address leads you to a door in a whitewashed wall with no windows on the first and second floors. Higher up there are chain linked windows allowing people to peer out but not allowing those outside to see in. You think you see a pair of eyes staring at you. But you are not sure. It is hot and you are impatient for someone to respond to your ringing the doorbell.

Then the door opens. But no one is there. You peer down a long corridor of whitewashed walls hung with beautifully patterned red and blue rugs. A fan whirls over-head in a central room at the end of the hall. The smell of incense fills the air.

If you go on in, turn to page 80.

If you ring the bell again and wait, turn to page 79.

You agree to meet Anson in Morocco. He is delayed getting from the airport to downtown Tangiers and the walled inner city called the Medina. There has been a traffic accident. A donkey cart and a car have collided. Anson waits, growing more restless by the moment. Little does he know that at the precise moment he sits in his taxi under the warm North African sun you are just entering the whitewashed house in the Medina. You could use his support, but time is slipping by. You have decided to go into the house alone.

Turn to page 80.

The plane to Paris is hijacked exactly eleven minutes after it takes off. Five people wearing masks and waving guns announce that they are taking the plane to China!

The captain attempts to calm everyone down by assuring the passengers that everything will be done according to the hijackers' demands. But that only seems to add to the passengers' panic.

The plane does not have enough fuel for such a long trip, and the pilot has to land in Greece at the Athens airport.

After landing, the plane is surrounded by police and military vehicles. The hijackers call for everyone to listen up: "We need a hostage. If someone volunteers to come with us, we will let the others go. We promise not to harm the hostage. We will let the hostage go after we get to China. Are there any volunteers?"

If you volunteer to be a hostage, turn to page 82.

If you remain quiet, turn to page 83.

58

You decide to rent a car, drive to the coast, and take a boat from Gibraltar to Tangiers. The drive is uneventful, but once aboard the hydrofoil speeding across the Strait of Gibraltar, your calm is disrupted when the cabin speaker asks if there is a passenger named Nabooti aboard.

The familiar shudder of fear ripples your body. You remain quiet and look at the deck, studying the drops of spray that collect on the smooth wooden planks. Someone is on board who can only mean you harm.

The hydrofoil completes its trip to Tangiers. You don't get off, but you buy a return trip ticket to Spain. You hope whoever it was will realize that you have decided to give up your search. It was a wild-goose chase after all, you tell yourself. Peter and Lucy can take it from here.

The End

60

It was a mistake to suggest Paris as the meeting place. Anson got off the plane and went to the address of a cafe given to him by a person posing as an agent of Nabooti. He drops out of sight. POOF, VANISHED! You are once again on your own. This is too much. Your friend Anson is more important than any jewels. You decide to give up this search for the jewels and find Anson.

The End

You hesitate for just a moment. The leader does not wait but fires a gas-loaded pen in your face. You choke on the small cloud of dense gas, feel your senses numbing, and fall to Earth.

The three men load you roughly into the helicopter and zoom off.

When you come to, your head feels heavy, your eyes sting, and you are dizzy.

If you pretend to still be unconscious hoping that you can figure out some plan for dealing with these people, turn to page 86.

If you decide to deal with the situation immediately and try to strike some bargain, turn to page 87.

There is no sense in fighting. You drop the pistol to the ground. You raise your hands above your head, and you say, "OK, it's up to you. No fight. Lead the way."

Soon you are in the helicopter scurrying across the French countryside. One of the people turns and says, "Join us. We want you to work for us. We will pay you anything you want, but the important thing is to help us."

What is going on? Everyone seems to want your help. First it was Peter and Lucy. Then the man on the plane. Then Molotawa. As far as you are concerned, you need

help yourself. "What for? Why me?"

Your captor speaks, "The Jewels of Nabooti are perhaps the most important force in the modern world. They are powerful tools that can be used for good or evil. The people you are dealing with pretend they support the good side. They are liars. We are on the side of good. They are evil. Whoever holds the jewels can either do great good or cause great harm in the world. Join us."

But, who in the world are these people? You haven't the faintest clue. Now you are really worried. Who knows what to believe? But the reality is that you are a prisoner of desperate people.

If you join them, turn to page 84.

If you stall for time, turn to page 85.

You dash past the car, ignoring the man, and lose yourself in the crowd of people walking on the narrow sidewalk.

Sometimes it is a good idea to stop and think, and other times it is best to act. This is the time for reflection. Too much has gone on without planning. You are not in control. Now you must take matters back into your own hands.

Stopping at an intersection, you decide to walk into a park across the street, sit down, and make some plans.

Go on to page 66.

You find a quiet sunny spot, and sit on an unoccupied bench. You are hungry, but there is no time for food now, so you stretch your legs and arms, gaze at the sky, and think about what has happened so far. You jot these facts in your notebook:

1. Jewels of Nabooti stolen in Boston.
2. Letter from rug merchant demanding jewels.
3. Mysterious man on plane to Paris.
4. Molotawa in cafe with story about world peace.
5. An address in Morocco for information to follow the lost jewels.
6. A lot of people apparently after the jewels and you.

Conclusions:

DANGER
TROUBLE
CONFUSION

What is the next step? Back to the cafe to Molotawa or on to Morocco?

If it's back to talk with Molotawa, turn to page 88.

If it's on to Morocco, turn to page 89.

You have to stoop to enter. Sitting in the darkness is an old man. He is dressed in a simple, worn, khaki shirt and shorts. He is barefoot.

"Come in. Sit down." The old man does not even look up at you. His eyes are closed.

I have been waiting for you." He hands you a black cup with six chicken bones, two parrot feathers, and the tooth of a hyena.

"Throw these on the floor." You do as he commands, and the bones, feathers, and tooth form a pattern that is barely discernible in the dim light.

He opens his eyes and studies the pattern of the objects, then he says, "The Mountains of the Moon bear the secret of your search. But, so too do the upper waters of the great Zaire River. Look for the sign of the snake and the mask of the crocodile." Then he closes his eyes and leans back in a trance.

If you go to the Mountains of the Moon,
turn to page 90.

If you travel to the headwaters of the Zaire River,
turn to page 92.

You are adventurous, no doubt about that. A shaman is another word for a witch doctor.

You and Ouobessa rent an old Land Rover and drive out of the city. Within twenty kilometers of Dakar the road turns to the deep, red claylike earth so characteristic of equatorial Africa. Huge trees, some over thirty meters in height, shade the road.

"Road not the best, but we will be there by nightfall. Want some papaya juice?" It is Ouobessa talking. You shake your head, then change your mind, and accept a cup of the sweet, odd-tasting juice.

The Land Rover bumps along, and finally you arrive at a small village. There are twenty-three circular huts of roughly the same size. They surround a slightly larger hut. It is to this larger hut that you and Ouobessa head.

Go back to page 67.

Where should you look for the Nabooti tribe? There isn't any listing in the phone directory, no fax number, no e-mail address, not even a website. They are a nomadic tribe that wanders from the northern part of Senegal to Chad to the edge of the Sahara.

An article in the local newspaper catches your eye. The Nabooti tribe was reported heading toward Lake Chad.

You rent a twin-engine light plane and fly to the huge, shallow lake just south of the Sahara. The pilot swoops down low over the water, and an enormous flock of flamingos take off turning the horizon pink.

You read the guidebook you brought with you and it warns the traveler,

"DON'T SWIM IN THIS LAKE! IT IS FILLED WITH PARASITES THAT CAN KILL YOU!"

Go on to the next page.

Your plane crosses airspace held by a revolutionary guerrilla group. You are forced to land at an unused airstrip near the old French town called Fort Lamy, home of the Foreign Legion.

When you land the plane, you are surrounded by people with rifles pointed at you.

If you try to take off again, turn to page 94.

If you get out of the plane and hold your hand up in a signal of peace, turn to page 95.

Dakar is beautiful and confusing. Old buildings from past ages stand next to modern hotels and offices. Certain high vantage points give a magnificent view of the Atlantic Ocean and the island of Goree, the infamous gathering point in the slave trade. Tall, handsome people in western dress and African garb move about. Flowers and palms line the streets. You begin at the university by examining the index cards in the library catalogue files. Nabooti is listed as a tribe, a religion, a man, a region, and a place. You could spend your life in the library. But you want action.

There is a listing in the tourist guide for a trip to the beautiful beaches and Club Nabooti.

If you take the trip, turn to page 96.

If you rent a car and drive to Club Nabooti by yourself, turn to page 98.

INCREDIBLE! There in the coat pocket are the Jewels of Nabooti! How did they get there? Who put them there?

But, that is not important. There they are, bright, incredible, powerful, mysterious.

The old man smiles, takes them from your hand before you can do a thing, and says, "You have done well in returning the Jewels of Nabooti to their rightful owners. Blessings will befall you. Your life will be rich with friends and adventure. Do not wonder how they came to you. It is all in the magic of the jewels. You were their messenger and helper. We thank you."

As the old man speaks you see him change form. He becomes younger, taller, and glows with a gentle gold radiance. You did the right thing. He is the king. The leader. The source of good.

The End

Guns are trouble. Certainly a gun can be useful if you are attacked, but it may invite violence. You have chosen to take this weapon. Be warned, it is dangerous!

Raoul hands you a compact black automatic. He shows you how to load it, points out the safety catch, tells you it has eight cartridges in a clip, and cautions you to use it only when it is really necessary. You hold the gun in your hand and aim it at a picture on the wall opposite you. Then you slip it in your pocket.

Raoul suggests that you and he should make contact with the secret African People's Federation. It consists of politicians, writers, philosophers, and exiles from many of the African countries south of the Sahara. You would like to meet them, but you are anxious to get on your way. Delays are eating up time.

If you go to meet the African People's Federation, turn to page 97.

If you skip the proposed meeting and push on for Morocco, turn to page 100.

You pretend to fumble in your pocket, while you look for an escape route. The old man sees through your ruse. He stamps the ground and kicks angrily. You dash for a rear door and burst through.

The door leads to a beautiful courtyard garden containing a calm dark pool filled with lotus flowers. A fat greasy man on the other side of the pool is sharpening scimitars on an old stone wheel. He takes one unsmiling look, grabs a knife and walks toward you.

What the heck, you think. That pool is looking pretty good! You take a running leap and dive in, much to the fat man's surprise. He tries to motion you to stop.

You ignore him and turn to swim, when you notice a pair of eyes just above the surface coming toward you. Crocodile. More eyes converge on you as you thrash to escape the oncoming open jaws. Too late.

The End

You don't like guns. Raoul is upset that you won't take one, but it's up to you. Now what?

He suggests lunch in a little restaurant on the Left Bank because, according to him, "It is always best to begin difficult tasks without the burden of hunger."

The restaurant is named Albert's. It is pleasant, the food tastes good, and the owner is friendly.

When the meal is done, you pick up the check. At the bottom of the check is written:

LEAVE BY THE BACK DOOR. TURN LEFT AT RUE PELICAN, RIGHT AT RUE FUGERE. WAIT UNTIL YOU ARE CONTACTED. RG

Raoul has gone to wash his hands. He does not return. You are alone.

Do you follow the instructions in the note? If so, turn to page 101.

If you wait for Raoul to return, turn to page 103.

SECRET ONLINE ENDING

If you do not trust the anonymous note and search for Raoul instead, go to www.cyoa.com/nabooti9221.htm

Once again you push the doorbell. It is hot and muggy, and you scuffle your shoes in the cobbled stones of the street. You hear the sound of footsteps within, and the door opens wider.

A young man wearing a colorful djellaba stands in front of you. He wears a curved scimitar at his side. A friendly smile spreads over his face.

"Come in, do come in. I am sorry to have kept you waiting so long."

There is something strange about him. Maybe it's his accent or the look on his face. You can't be sure, but it seems phony. You enter slowly and cautiously.

Then it hits you!

The person in front of you is PETER! What in the world is he doing here in Morocco dressed in this crazy djellaba?

To find out, turn to page 104.

80

You take a cautious step into the hallway. It is noticeably cooler inside. Another step, then two more. There is only the sound of your shoes on the red tiles of the floor and the whining of the fan. The door behind you closes on oiled hinges. You stop, look about, and then peer into a room off to the side.

Then it happens! The floor falls away under you, and you spin dizzily down and down, coming to a nasty crash on a sodden, damp earthen floor. It is pitch-black. There are no exits; there is no food, no water. You are doomed.

The End

Your legs feel rubbery as you walk down the stairs from the plane. The sun reflecting on the runway hurts your eyes. How crazy can you be? What purpose is there in volunteering to be a hostage? But then, hunting for the Jewels of Nabooti is dangerous, too. One way or another, your life is filled with adventure.

Finally you are seated in a fast-moving touring car and driven to the opposite end of the runway. Your captors are silent. The two women are firm and businesslike. The man reeks of garlic. You are led to another plane.

Just as you are getting near the steps up to the plane, a Greek army captain shouts, "Run for it. We've got you covered."

If you run for it, turn to page 108.

If you keep on going up the steps of the plane, turn to page 107.

There is silence in the aircraft. No hands are raised. The hijackers look from face to face. The leader speaks again,

"All right. You have exactly five minutes to produce a hostage. Then we will choose." He looks at his watch.

You think about volunteering, but you still can't get your hand up in the air. Minutes tick by. The leader speaks. "We are losing precious time. We will take all of you with us. The plane will be refueled. You had your chance."

It is as he says. The plane is refueled. It takes off and heads toward China. Two escort planes fly behind it. What a mess! You are never going to get to Morocco. Not only that, but what are your chances of getting off this plane alive? Sit tight and hope for the best.

The End

For several moments you scratch at a piece of rubber lining on the Plexiglas window of the helicopter. No one says anything, and the helicopter just grinds through the sky.

Then you turn slowly in your seat, face the person who spoke to you, and you reply, "I need proof of what you say. How do I know which group to believe? For all I know, you are all bandits."

The leader speaks again. "You must have faith. Believe in us. You will see."

But you remember all too clearly the machine gun bullets ripping through the car. That is no way to fight for good—trying to kill people.

You say, "Look, I'm out of this. I don't want any more jewels, any more trips, and any more trouble. Just let me go back to the United States. I won't cause any of you trouble."

They actually agree and let you go!

When you arrive at Boston's Logan Airport, you are once again met by Peter and Lucy. They beg you to return to Europe and continue the search for the jewels.

Turn to page 9.

As you gaze down at the green country below you, you see an orange flash. It looks like a Fourth of July rocket. But it is speeding toward you!

BALOOM! SCROSH!

It's all over. The rocket hits the helicopter. You are finished.

The End

You keep your eyes shut pretending to be asleep. The three men discuss what they will do next. You hear mention of Monsieur Rigolade, a famous French politician. You are amazed that he is involved in this activity. What in the world can be his motives for associating with the Nabooti group?

One man says, "Let's throw this spare baggage out . . . no use to us . . . knows nothing."

With a start, you realize that they are talking about you. You sit up.

"Hey, wait a minute! Slow down! I know plenty. I can help."

The three men turn and grin at you. Their ploy worked. You have just admitted knowing about the Jewels of Nabooti.

"OK. Keep talking. Help us and you won't get hurt."

"What do you want?" you ask.

"We want you to cable your cousins, tell them to get here right away. Then we will move on to the next step."

If you agree to cable Peter and Lucy,
turn to page 115.

If you argue with them, turn to page 116.

"Hey, I'll give you what you want. Let's be reasonable." You are scared but pretend to be tough.

"We want the jewels. Pure, simple, straight. The jewels, now!"

Thinking fast, you respond with the following, "OK, but only I can get them. The diamonds are in Morocco. The rubies are in Boston. Without me, you won't get anywhere."

It's a bluff. Maybe it will work. They tell you to choose where to go first.

If you choose Morocco, turn to page 117.

If you choose Boston, turn to page 118.

Molotawa seems to be the key to the Jewels of Nabooti. You circle back to the cafe, find the waiter, ask him to get in touch with Molotawa, and wait in a small back room next to the kitchen.

Molotawa arrives, and you agree with him to go on to Senegal to meet the fabled Nabooti tribe.

But, once again, just as you get up to go, a man jumps up and lunges at you, knife in hand. It is a nightmare repeat of a few hours ago.

You step to the side, put your foot out, and the would-be attacker trips. The knife clatters to the floor.

Molotawa is grim. He speaks.

"You bring bad luck. I fear you. We must separate now."

If you press him to take you with him to the Nabooti tribe, turn to page 109.

If you apologize and leave by yourself, turn to page 110.

As you sit in the warm sunshine deciding about going to Morocco, you catch sight of what looks like a small plump girl with an odd-looking dog. She runs up to you, laughing happily, and hands you the leash. She runs away. When you look down, you realize that the dog is a mechanical dog, not a real one. Without warning, it explodes into a thousand brilliant shards of metal. The explosion finishes you off.

UGH! What a horrible way to go.

The End

The Mountains of the Moon are in the Ruwenzori Mountain chain. Only a few years ago, these high peaks were snow-covered, a truly rare sight in tropical Africa. But now with the climate warming, sub-Saharan Africa is losing the snow that once crowned its highest peaks.

You and Ouobessa travel by plane, truck, and finally, foot, until you stand at the base of the highest peak in the Ruwenzori. The tropical forest is brilliant, shining green, and the flowering plants flash yellow and red. Giant ferns and huge plants surround you and Ouobessa.

You have heard that there is a guide service to the

peaks of the Mountains of the Moon. But when you reach the small, wooden hut with the rusty metal roof, no one is there. On a wooden table inside the hut is a map of the main peaks showing routes and several overnight huts. One is marked in red. Underneath it is a crude line drawing of four jewels.

You look at each other. A rat scurries across the earthen floor of the hut. Far off there is the sound of drums. The beat is steady, rich, and hypnotic.

You decide to wait for the guide.

Turn to page 111.

The Zaire River is a mighty, wide river flowing from the highlands of Central Africa down to the sea. Many tributaries run into the Zaire. Cataracts and falls make journeys on parts of the Zaire difficult, and floating water lilies provide an eerie beauty. Crocodiles lie half-submerged, ready to snap at the unwary. Hand-hewn canoes called *pirogues* are poled by fishermen. River steamers loaded with people and goods travel up and down the navigable parts of the river.

You and Ouobessa fly to Kinshasa and book passage on the *River King*. You climb aboard just as it casts off. The big paddle wheels churn the brown water. You watch them, almost hypnotized at the sight.

Turn to the next page.

Four days later, you and Ouobessa disembark at Leelengalli, the end of the line. Now you must travel by a small boat paddled by men from the village.

Four more days of endless travel lead you deeper into the jungle. You have heard tales of a man called Kurtz. It is rumored that he holds the Jewels of Nabooti.

Turn to page 125.

Release the brakes!

Kick the rudder pedals hard left!

Push the throttles full forward!

Bump down the strip. Bullets rip through the thin metal skin of the plane.

You make it into the air and dash for the border away from Chad. But your plane runs out of fuel and you land in a desolate, almost desert area.

You have very little water, no food, and no little prince to help you.

The End

You strike a bargain with the leader of this band of cutthroats.

They lead you to the Nabooti tribe camped peacefully on the shores of Lake Chad.

The jewels have been returned. The power of peace is flowing in the world.

Congratulations on a job well done.

The End

Club Nabooti is jammed. People from Brazil, Germany, Japan, Canada, and other countries, large and small, crowd the gigantic swimming pool, occupy all the tables in the outdoor restaurant, fill the tennis courts, and cover the beach. The flash of credit cards and the jingle of change on the gaming tables underline that this place is for the very rich.

A man invites you into his office. When you mention the Jewels of Nabooti, he laughs, slaps you on the back, and says, "Sure, we had them, but we sold them to pay for the new addition to the club."

You don't think that's very funny.

The End

Seventeen floors above the city of Paris is a room in a new skyscraper. It looks out on Notre Dame.

One person, an African named Patrice, sits at a large desk. He does not smile. He points to chairs and you and Raoul sit. Then he speaks in a slow and precise fashion.

"The jewels are safe. You may give up the search. Here is proof." He hands you a cable from Peter and Lucy. It reads:

RETURN BOSTON. ALL WELL. SEARCH OVER.
P & L

The End

Club Nabooti is a front for the headquarters of the Nabooti Peace Group. Since people from all over the world vacation here, it is not difficult to carry on their worldwide campaign for peace. People pretending to be vacationers are really secret agents who are trained here for missions all over the world. This lush resort is really the headquarters and training camp of the world's most powerful peace group.

You are welcomed, asked to join the search team, and given the secret codes used by all members of the Nabooti group to ward off danger.

Your efforts so far have earned you respect and a membership in a peace team. It is a great honor.

The End

100

You were told by Peter and Lucy that Morocco was the key. And when you check into your room in Morocco, what a surprise! A note at the hotel desk tells you that Peter and Lucy are in Room 12! They flew direct from Boston. Raoul is not surprised, but then, being a good police officer, he is never surprised at anything people do.

Peter and Lucy explain that a message told them to go to Morocco or else you would be killed. Peter says, "But now that we are here we have other leads to follow. On the back of an envelope pushed under Lucy's door the other night were two addresses. Both are here in Morocco!"

If you go with Lucy and Raoul to the first address, turn to page 129.

If you go with Peter and Raoul to the second address, turn to page 131.

You search for Raoul. The waiter, who is busy wiping bread crumbs off the tablecloth, says he left in a hurry through the back door.

You walk up and down Rue Fugere for more than half an hour. Then a car pulls to a stop. The window is rolled down. A hand slips out. A piece of paper flutters to the ground.

Turn to the next page.

GO TO THE EIFFEL TOWER. TAKE THE ELEVATOR
TO THE TOP. RG

Should you do this? You don't know who these
people are. It's like a treasure hunt, but the results could
spell D-E-A-T-H.

If you go on to the Eiffel Tower, turn to page 130.

If you double back to the restaurant, turn to page 46.

Raoul reappears behind you. He drops a small packet into your lap.

You look at each other in dismay.

Inside are the Jewels of Nabooti. But they've been crushed into small shards, now worthless both as priceless gems and the repository of magical power.

The End

"Peter, what in the world are you doing here? I thought you and Lucy were going to stay in Boston where you would be safe. This is some surprise!"

Peter puts a finger to his lips and indicates silence. Then he leads the way into the house. You cross the large, comfortable living room and enter the study. It is filled with large cushions on the floor, bookshelves, and a very ornate desk made of carved wood. He is standing in front of a large oriental painting. With a slight forward movement, Peter leans against a wooden panel in the wall. Noiselessly, the wall slides back revealing a stairway lit by three small lamps. Once again he beckons you to follow, and again he puts a finger to his lips in the universal sign for quiet and secrecy.

The steps are carpeted. There is no sound as you descend into the gloom. This is really too much!

Then you are standing in a room filled with seventeen people. They range in age from very young to very old. There are people of all colors—black, yellow, brown, and white—in the room.

Turn to page 106.

Standing in the center are two figures cloaked in white robes. Before them is a box. In the box are the Jewels of Nabooti!

One of the people is Lucy. The other the African named Molotawa.

"Welcome. You have passed the test. You are courageous and dedicated. We offer you membership in the International Tribe of Nabooti. This is an honor few people ever hear of—fewer still receive. Step forward, please."

As you step forward, you realize that your life has changed forever. You are part of a worldwide organization fighting for world peace.

Good luck.

The End

It is too dangerous to attempt an escape. You follow the other passengers onto the plane, wishing all the while that you were going back home.

The plane takes off, heading for China. The leader, a beautiful brunette with intense green eyes, sits down next to you. Leaning forward, she whispers, "I can read minds. It is a gift. I know that you are searching for the Jewels of Nabooti. You must give up the search. The jewels will destroy those who seek them."

You stare at the woman, wondering if she is mad. Does she really want to help you or is she your enemy? Terrified, you shrink down into your chair and close your eyes. You drift into a nightmare in which the leader's eyes turn into gorgeous but deadly green snakes that slither around your throat choking you. You gasp for breath as the plane hurtles through the air to China.

The End

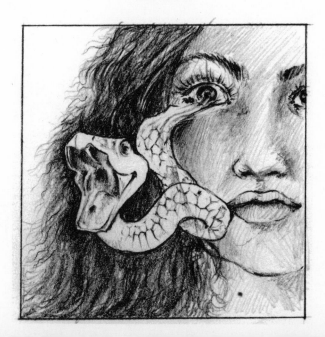

Duck! Sprint! Crouch low! Bullets whip over your head. Then you are safe behind a Greek army jeep. The hijackers are in the plane, but the army squad shoots out the tires. It's all over for them.

How about you? You've had enough adventure for a time.

Should you stay in Greece for a rest? If so, turn to page 113.

Should you go back home? If so, turn to page 114.

"I must go with you. I bring no bad luck. Give me another chance." You stand there waiting for his reply.

"I am afraid of the spirits who fight against us. You must prove that you are not a spy, an informer, an enemy."

It is not easy to prove anything, especially that you are his friend and not his enemy.

"What do you suggest, Molotawa?"

He thinks for a while and says, "I will give you two tasks to perform. You choose which one you want. Your choice will reveal who you really are."

Then Molotawa draws from his pocket a piece of paper folded neatly and carefully. He unfolds it and points to it.

"Task one involves the removal of certain objects from a bank safe. It is simple, but perhaps dangerous." You look at the paper. It is a map showing an underground tunnel leading into a large building. An X marks a row of vaults in the basement.

You say nothing.

"Task two involves helping one of our men to escape. His name is Ramolt, and he is wanted all over Europe. We have him concealed in a secret hideout. If you accept this task, you will lead him along a dangerous escape route. Your life will be threatened as well, but if you succeed, you will be rewarded beyond your wildest dreams."

If you choose task one, turn to page 119.

If you choose task two, turn to page 122.

110

Speak about bad luck! First the Jewels of Nabooti and now Molotawa are the messengers of trouble. You want no part of them. You shake hands and mumble a few words of regret about the recent events. Then you leave the restaurant.

The street is crowded, and you get away without incident.

Your pace slows and you begin to relax. Then you feel a tug at your arm. What now? But it is only a monkey on a chain with a tin can in his hand. The chain leads to an organ grinder. The organ grinder smiles, nods, and says, "A few francs, perhaps?"

You search your pocket and come up with a handful of coins that you drop in the tin cup.

No sooner does the clank of the coins stop, than the organ grinder says, "Run for your life."

Turn to page 120.

The afternoon shadows soon fall across the small glade. It is dark underneath the giant ferns and trees. The drums have not ceased. Occasionally you hear the sounds of birds and other animals.

"Ouobessa, I don't like this. I mean, what are we doing here? We don't even know what we are looking for."

Ouobessa turns, stares at the darkening jungle, and says, "It is too early to tell."

You point to the map on the table and the drawing of the jewels. "OK, so we head there, but what then? I mean, way up in the mountains. Look, the place marked is at the 14,000-foot level."

He agrees, and the two of you choose ice axes, ropes, packs, and crampons from the supply stacked in the corner of the room. How weird to have to prepare for an alpine climb in Africa!

You trudge off, following the path through the ferns. The crampons clank in the pack. The rope feels heavy on your shoulders.

After an hour you notice the ferns are gone, and scrub brush dots the landscape. Rocks and cliffs soar in front of you. The trail changes to rocks you must scramble up. Then you are on a cliff. You and Ouobessa inch up the face, roped together. The going is difficult.

Yowee! You slip. Knuckles smash against rough rock. Blood bubbles to the surface. The rope attached to Ouobessa tautens, stretches, and holds. You are safe. You huddle against the rock face catching your breath.

Turn to page 112.

At the top of the cliff, you leave the rock face, cross snowfields, and climb steeply. The sun beats down on you. It reflects on the snow and blinds you. You have no sunglasses. Then you see it; it is a small mountain hut made out of aluminum. It's an emergency shelter.

Across the doorway are three chicken bones and two dead mice. Ouobessa screams, "Stop. Don't touch. This is magic. It is a curse and a warning. It means it is death to enter."

If you ignore the warning and go into the hut,
turn to page 123.

If you heed Ouobessa and refuse to enter,
turn to page 124.

Greece is beautiful. Clouds sail above the Acropolis; the sea is golden in the afternoon sun. You give up this frantic chase for the fabled jewels. You even decide to take a job in Athens working for the English language newspaper called the *Amphora*.

The End

114

Going back home means giving up. You know that, but what can you really do? One person alone trying to find the Jewels of Nabooti is impossible.

With a feeling of regret, you fly to Boston and taxi out to where you and Peter and Lucy met to discuss the problem. But when you arrive at their home, they are not there. A note on the kitchen table sends you to an address in downtown Boston.

Go to page 127.

The cable to Peter and Lucy asks them to meet you in Paris immediately. But they are not at home. There is no reply. Your captors bind and gag you and drop you in a trash bin behind a French fast food shop called L'Express.

UGH! The smell of fries, greasy meat, and stale bread overpowers you.

But luck is with you. A mangy dog nosing around for a free meal discovers you and barks. You are freed just before the trash masher picks up the bin.

Brush off the fries, sponge away the mustard. You are free, alive, and well. But you have had enough. You give up the search and go home.

The End

This was one time that you shouldn't have argued. They open the cabin door and push you out!

PLOP!

Right into a farm pond. Wet but safe.

The End

Arriving at the address in Morocco, you push into the shop, yell for help, and dive to the floor. You are knocked out by a sharp blow to the head.

When you wake up, there is no one there. You are groggy but otherwise unharmed. You search your pockets. Only one thing is missing: the slip of paper with Peter and Lucy's telephone number in Boston! Pinned to your chest is a note. It says, *Merci!* (That's French for thanks!)

"Those fools." You grin like an idiot. "They are probably on their way to the United States right now! I'm glad I memorized the address of the rug merchant."

Now to find the rug merchant.

Turn back to page 47.

118

An international airline strike has stopped all planes from taking off. While waiting in the airport, you get a note to contact the police. In good faith you go up to a gendarme standing by the counter at the newsstand. The minute you identify yourself, the gendarme becomes suspicious.

The gendarme takes you to an office where a fat officer sits at a desk munching on french fries. He holds your passport in his greasy hand, compares the picture with a fax in his other hand. You are able to peek and see the words, "Dangerous fugitive, arrest immediately!"

You are about to protest that this is surely a case of mistaken identity, but they have you in handcuffs before you can get two words out.

You are arrested, charged with plotting against the French government, and put in prison.

It will be a long legal battle to get you out.

The End

The "removal of certain objects" Molotawa speaks of is a bank robbery. The folded paper reveals plans for using a sewer tunnel to gain access to the vaults of the Banque de France.

Molotawa grins, slaps you on the back, and says, "Just as I thought. A crook at heart. We'll do well together." Now you're really in a jam.

The End

You turn, frantically looking at the faces in the crowd. Where is the danger coming from?

"Run for your life!" the organ grinder shouts again. He waves his arms. The monkey shrieks. A large black van cruises to a halt near the man and his monkey. The tinted-glass windows prevent you from seeing who is in it. You are frozen with fear.

Once again the sharp, loud cry "Run for your life!" pierces the air. People stop walking. They look at you, the organ grinder, then the black van.

You can hear breathing. The side door of the van opens slowly. Out step six men dressed in black, holding something long and shiny in their hands.

Go on to the next page.

You feel the pounding of your heart, the beat of blood in your veins. You begin to move, but the crowd seems to block you. It becomes somewhat like a living fence.

"Let me go, let me go!" You scream in English and then in French. But no one pays any attention to you.

The six men form a small circle. Three have guitars, one a saxophone, one a flute, and the other an African drum.

Run for Your Life is a rock-and-roll band. They are putting on a street theater concert for publicity.

Relax. Enjoy the music!

The End

122

Ramolt is the code name for a leader of the Nabooti Peace Group. He is hiding from the authorities, who fear him because he has the power to lead revolutions. People follow him. They believe in him. You are asked to accompany him by train in an attempt to escape and return to Africa.

He is one of the Jewels of Nabooti. The jewels are four famous people who lead the fight for world peace. The real jewels are valuable but unimportant.

You have made a brave choice. Good luck.

The End

You cross the threshold. Nothing happens. Your eyes grow accustomed to the gloom. It is a small hut with enough room for six people in sleeping bags—a typical high-altitude mountaineering hut.

There is a low table in the center. You and Ouo-bessa approach it.

There they are. The fabled Jewels of Nabooti, two rubies as red as the glistening tongue of a cobra and two diamonds that shimmer like sunlight reflecting on a mirror.

You and Ouobessa stare in disbelief. You reach out to touch them.

ZONK! You are hit with a bolt of lightning. The energy in the lightning momentarily paralyzes you. The Jewels of Nabooti vanish. The sky is clear of clouds.

You will never lay hands on the jewels.

The End

Ouobessa says, "It is not good. A curse like this means that we are still being followed. One of us will go for help. One of us will stay here."

You hesitate but finally agree. With the flip of a coin, you decide who stays watch and who goes down for more help.

You win. You go down the mountain, but you slip on an ice pitch and tumble into a deep crevasse. There is no way out. Ouobessa sits alone and waits for you.

The End

"Mister Kurtz? He's dead. A penny for the old guy."
It is an African talking. You stare at a ramshackle
building surrounded by the jungle.

"But he left a package for people he said would one
day come. It is there. Perhaps you are the ones."

The package contains the Jewels of Nabooti.
Wrapped in old newspapers are the four stones. They
glow with an inner warmth that makes you feel good
inside. There is beauty and power in these stones. They
are symbols of strength and peace.

The End

The stranger is an old man with kind eyes. He smiles.

"We have been trying to reach you for several weeks now. Allow me to introduce myself. I am Jean Pierre Borel, and I come from Morocco. I believe that you want these."

Mr. Borel takes your hand and puts four small paper-wrapped packets in your palm. You stare at them, not knowing quite what to do. Then you open one. Wow! There it is. A huge diamond. A ruby. Another ruby and the fourth, the other diamond. Borel sits still, smiling at you. You speak.

"But, I mean, where did they come from? How did you get them? Why are you giving them to me?" Mr. Borel holds up his hand as if to stop you. Then he answers.

"My friend, questions are not always necessary. Accept the gift. Do what you must do."

You don't know what to say. There are the jewels in your hand. The search is over . . . or maybe it's just begun.

The End

The address turns out to be the Museum of Fine Arts. A large sign out front announces the exhibit of the fabled Jewels of Nabooti—a recent loan to the museum by an anonymous group.

You notice four or five children outside the museum wearing Nabooti T-shirts. They are listening to a CD player and doing a strange dance. The music blares "Do the Nabooti," a new hit dance tune.

The End

The surf roars in and crashes on the beaches just below the jutting cliffs called the Pillars of Hercules. The crash of waves is not only on the beach! The crew members yell, "Watch out, look out for that wave!" But they have forgotten the treacherous rollers of the Atlantic that pound the shores of Africa. The boat rolls violently and is tossed up into the air by a giant wave. You cry out, "Helllp-HELLLP!"

The boat smashes to pieces in the milk-white surf. All hands are lost.

The End

You, Lucy, and Raoul arrive at the address, and all three of you look at one another with fear and excitement.

You are met by a giant in a flowing gray and brown robe. He glares at you and pushes you into the shop. Before you can do anything, the three of you are handcuffed and gagged.

"You will be held as hostages for the Jewels of Nabooti. We set a six-day time period. Then it is off with your heads."

Five days pass. No word.

This is the middle of the sixth day.

The End

Once atop the Eiffel Tower you look out on the beautiful city of Paris. In the slanting light of late afternoon it sparkles like a thousand jewels. The sun is reflected from panes of glass. They shimmer like radiant gems for a minute, then the sun dips lower.

The Jewels of Nabooti were finally about beauty and peace. And beauty is all around us—if we just look and really see.

The End

"Pete, what do you think this is all about?"

Peter doesn't answer but gives a grin and a shrug of the shoulders.

Raoul is anxious to go. When you arrive at the address, you are surprised to see that it is a small palace on the outskirts of Tangiers. Guards with dogs surround the palace. You are immediately allowed to enter.

You stroll down long marble halls lined with fountains. Your footsteps echo as you are led deeper and deeper into the palace.

You are in a large room. Eleven people stand around a small table. On the table is a three-foot-long curved sword with four jewels in the hilt. They are the Jewels of Nabooti. The sword glows with a mysterious light. It rises off the table, glides through the air, and comes to rest in your hand.

You are the new guardian of the Jewels of Nabooti. The chosen leader for peace and justice.

The End

GLOSSARY

Acropolis – The Acropolis is a famous hill in the center of Athens. It means "Sacred Rock" and is home to four ancient monuments dating back to antiquity. The most important of the four is the Parthenon. The Parthenon was dedicated to Athena Parthenos, the patron goddess of Athens, at the height of the ancient Greek civilization. It was completed in 432 B.C.

Djellabah – A garment that is long and loose with full sleeves and a hood. It is commonly worn by men in the Middle East, especially in Muslim countries.

Interpol – Interpol is an acronym for International Criminal Police Organization. It is an international intelligence agency that allows countries around the world to work together to collect secret information about actual or potential enemies.

Lake Chad – A shallow lake in north central Africa bordering the countries of Chad, Cameron, Niger and Nigeria. Europeans first explored Lake Chad in 1823.

Medina – The old, non-European section of an Arab city in North Africa.

Mountains of the Moon – The Mountains of the Moon are the nickname of the Ruwenzori Mountains between Uganda and Zaire. Some of the waters from the Ruwenzori help feed the Nile River.

Pirogue – A pirogue is a type of rustic canoe made from the hollowed out trunk of a tree.

Scimitar – A saber or sword having a curved blade with the sharp edge on the convex side (the side that bulges outward). Scimitars are common in Africa and the Middle East.

Senegal – A country in Western Africa on the Atlantic Coast. The population of Senegal is 7,899,000 and Dakar is the capital.

Shaman – A priest or priestess who uses magic for the purpose of curing the sick, finding hidden things, and directing events.

Straits of Hercules – The area at the mouth of the Mediterranean Sea separating the continents of Europe and Africa. The two points of land on either side of the Straits of Hercules are the Rock of Gibraltar in Spain and Jebel Musa in Morocco.

Tangiers – A city in northern Morocco at the west end of the Strait of Gibraltar. Tangiers was founded in Roman times. It has been controlled by a variety of countries, including Portugal and Great Britain. Its population is 307,000.

Tarantula – Any of various large, hairy spiders of the family Theraphosidae. Tarantulas are mainly found in the tropics. Their bite is painful, but their poison is not deadly to humans.

Dakar – Dakar is the capital and largest city in the country of Senegal. Dakar's population is 1,729,823. It borders the Atlantic Ocean and is the end point of a famous road rally starting in Paris.

CREDITS

Illustrator: Thananart Kornmaneeroj (Yo). Thananart was born in Chantaburi, Thailand. In addition to his artistic endeavors, he is an architect and a lecturer in the Department of Architecture at Chulalongkorn University.

Illustrator: Kachaine Chanchareon (Chaine). Kachaine is from Pra Juab Kirikan, Thailand. Kachaine works for Ayutthaya Building Co. Ltd. His drawings are enhanced by his experience in traditional Thai architecture.

Illustrator: Sorasith Butsingkhon (Kai). Sorasith was born in Roi Ed, Thailand and works for Geoartfact in Bangkok, Thailand.

Illustrator: Atthakrit Utahigarn (Note). Atthakrit hails from Prayao, Thailand and is a freelance artist with an architectural background.

This book was brought to life by a great group of people:

Shannon Gilligan, Publisher
Gordon Troy, General Counsel
Jason Gellar, Sales Director
Melissa Bounty, Senior Editor
Stacey Boyd, Designer

Thanks to everyone involved!

Buy the paperback version of this title and others at www.cyoa.com.

ABOUT THE AUTHOR

R. A. MONTGOMERY has hiked in the Himalayas, climbed mountains in Europe, scuba-dived in Central America, and worked in Africa. He lives in France in the winter, travels frequently to Asia, and calls Vermont home. Montgomery graduated from Williams College and attended graduate school at Yale University and NYU. His interests include macro-economics, geo-politics, mythology, history, mystery novels, and music. He has two grown sons, a daughter-in-law, and two granddaughters. His wife, Shannon Gilligan, is an author and noted interactive game designer. Montgomery feels that the new generation of people under 15 is the most important asset in our world.

For games, activities and other fun stuff, or to write to R. A. Montgomery, visit us online at CYOA.com